GOD
LOVES A
CHAMPION

🏆

TONY DRAKE

ISBN 978-1-63874-748-2 (paperback)
ISBN 978-1-63874-749-9 (digital)

Christian Faith Publishing, Inc.
832 Park Avenue
Meadville, PA 16335
www.christianfaithpublishing.com

Printed in the United States of America

CONTENTS

PREFACE

If you are reading this book, guess what? It is not by chance. Your spirit has connected with the spirit of the author through divine contact, and you have the spirit of a champion living on the inside of you. And right now at this appointed time, God has called for your spirit to wake up so that the champion inside you will come forth and shake the world upside down.

The harvest is abundant, but the laborers are few. The world offers a handsome reward to those who are willing to keep the people in the dark "far from the truth"—the truth of knowing who God is and why he loves us so much. The enemy's plan is to destroy God's creation, trying his best to convince the people that there is no God and we are our own gods by living our lives by our own rules and our own luck. The mission of the evil one is to keep convincing the people to chase the pipe dream—the so-called American dream, which I personally call the sleeper's dream. Chasing your feeling, chasing the wants of the flesh.

But the truth of the matter is, "God offers a bigger and everlasting reward" to those who are not ashamed of him openly confessing that he is the head of their life, willing to make a stand and die to the desires of the flesh. Making a stand to carry the torch of the good news of Jesus Christ is going to be one of the most challenged decision you will ever make in life.

Carry the torch of life—as the title of this book states, God loves a champion—because he really does. The bible talks about many champions who were chosen by God to serve and protect the people with uncompromising obedience to the voice of God, willing to lay down their own lives for God and the love of the people.

A spirit not everyone has or is willing to possess

The gift of being a champion comes from God, and the gift is not just for the receiver but for everyone around the chosen one. The gift is for God's purpose and his will alone. As one of God's champion, upon answering the call upon your life, you will have an assignment to fulfill: your life is not your own anymore as it belongs to the Lord and his purpose of why you were chosen to be a champion.

I would have never imagined that I would one day spend three years of my life to write a book to inspire others to wake up and seek out God's purpose in their life. The Holy Spirit would not let me rest until I picked up my pen and started writing this book, putting down on paper the words that were given to me that would uplift God's people.

> A quote from Bishop TD Jakes' *Get Ready, Get Ready, Get Ready.*

This book was written to give you a clear definition of the signs that you might have noticed within yourself. However, you were not comfortable with talking to no one about these strange feelings and new signs that you couldn't explain, so you just keep quiet about this part of your life—your newfound secret. As you embark on your search for your purpose in life as one of God's champions, always remember the promise that God made to those who choose to keep him first. "I'll never leave you nor forsake you." God's people, if you are fit for the kingdom, walk with me as we walk out our journey together as God's chosen champions.

Let us be a beacon of light to those in the dark. Let us put on the armor of God, daily prepared to be a soldier in God's army. We choose life in Christ with no other option. We must fight for this new generation so that Christ's death on the cross does not get lost in the shuffle of life. God's plan to save mankind from the devil is our mission. As his chosen champions of this generation, we will carry the torch till it's time to pass it on, and we will spread the news of the gospel till the world come to know our Lord and Savior Jesus Christ.

Grow to love God just as we did through the men and women of God before us.

ACKNOWLEDGMENTS

First of all, I would like to thank God for all that he has done in the past, present, and future. I would like to thank my Lord and Savior Jesus Christ because through him, we have been saved by grace, and I would like to thank the Holy Spirit for his spiritual guidance throughout my journey with my life in Christ. I am thankful for the anointing, the wisdom, the understanding, the discernment, and above all, the love God has shown me and continues to show me. I am that chosen vessel, the champion that God has appointed for this era to go out and bring others to the knowledge of Jesus Christ and also the love God has for his people.

There are some special people who need to be mentioned because you all were essential in one way or another with your words of encouragement, your lives exemplifying the holy characteristics of God's people. And I truly thank God for you all.

To my wife Evelyn Drake, it's been a rocky road. But through it all, God has kept us bonded like superglue, and I love you for hanging in there with me while God worked on molding me to be the man that he had plans for me to be someday.

To my sons Antonio Dante Thomas, DT Authentic; Anthony J. Drake Jr., keeping the AJD name going into the next generation; Arimes Dewayne Drake, a willing mind is a powerful tool to possess; and Timothy Upshaw, life is what you make it to be. You choose. In loving memory of my daughter Tonya Lynn Thomas. God has always had a plan for you to be one of his angels, and I thank him for allowing you to spend some time with us before you went home.

I would like to thank God for my mom Genette Byrd and my brothers Bobby, Ronnie, and Brandon. I would like to recognize the family and friends that God added in my life who were inspirational with the writing of this book.

I must admit I never had an older brother or sister, but to Larry and Arlene Moore, I have nothing but love for the both of you. You were truly God sent. Blessings and I love you both.

Dave and Joyce Meyer; Pastor Tony and Angie Gilmore; Rick and Judy Lamborn; Nathaniel and Cynthia Johnson; Gordon and Katie Madison; Barry and Sonya Carter; Angie Richardson, Roy and Kathy Lormis; and Donna Wheelis McNeil. Special thanks to Donna Chumley and Leslie Fox of Christian Faith Publishing, and the rest of the staff at CFP.

THE SPIRIT

E ven now, if you were to take a moment and reflect back on your life and how you were so different from everyone around you, it is only now you can see how God was molding and shaping you to be a vessel of honor. When everyone thought you were strange and weird because you dreamed big dreams and was always thinking outside the norm from everyone else, always acting out the role you wanted to be in life, imagining yourself living better than your present situation at that time, can I say this? You were not wrong for thinking this way. It was the Holy Spirit imputing your God-approved champion traits and his vision for your life.

Your destiny as well as my own evolved around our character-building lessons beginning with life's hard-knock journey, a journey that was filled with opposition and triumph, despair and hope. A lot of days filled with the pressure of giving in, but the heart of a champion that you possessed would not allow you to give up but endure.

Through the Holy Spirit, you were being trained to never give in—never giving up and taught to be a winner at all cost. You were being taught to listen to the inner voice of instruction and reasoning. That faint but silent voice that comes and goes in your time of need was then and is now the voice of the Holy Spirit. Chosen by God, there are three long-term lessons of faith building that we must be willing to accept the challenge of mastering in order to carry the torch of a champion.

Struggle, Sacrifice, and Strength

If you can come to grips of challenging yourself to master the 3S lessons now you are on your way of achieving something greater than you could have imagined within yourself.

We will dive deeper into the 3S's in later chapters throughout the book so that you will gain the understanding behind the lessons instead of just reading it and gathering information. Now, it's going to require some work and effort on your part, but you are not alone. It's going to feel like it at times, but you will have to remember this if God has called you to do a task for him. That means he is there with you even when you feel like giving up.

He made a promise that he will never leave nor forsake us, so this means we are never alone no matter what we are going through. But the lesson is not to trust in your own strength but trust in him through your own faith and only through your faith. Even for myself, I came to the realization that if I am going to win, if I am going to get through the challenges that I am facing, if I am going to carry the torch as one of God's esteemed champions, I must put all my trust in Jehovah Jirah—he is my provider.

Four decades into the future, I understand now the individual that everyone had seen back then is who God wanted them to see—someone not accepted by the world's standard but approved by God to be set apart to be revealed later as one of his champions. Even back then, I would question myself, *Why doesn't anyone like me? Why don't I ever get invited to the party?* But as I think back, I have to laugh now because God had a plan for myself and he was keeping me separated for a future purpose. God really, they were having so much fun back then.

But guess what, I missed it all to be where I am today, writing books for a living. And I would not trade it for anything even if I could. God has a really good sense of humor. How he will allow us to go through a lot of issues and uncontrollable temptations all for our good of gaining wisdom. Teaching us how to be well-mannered and well-behaved in the public eye, giving no room for humiliation and shame.

God is all knowing, and he knew in the end we will be thanking him for bringing us through it while we dreaded going through the beginning. However, I have to mention my wife in this book because she is my biggest supporter. Shout out to you, honey, Evelyn Drake. Something that my wife would always say to me, I had to put it in the book. "Never despise your small beginnings."

Predestined before birth, you were chosen—I was chosen—that one day we would represent the kingdom of God as one of God's esteemed champions. Despite our upbringings, whether it may have been well to do or poverty stricken, both lifestyles were designed by God. Fashioned in such a way, it only had to be God moving in a mighty way to elevate us, so only he would get the recognition from his people and the praise through you and me.

I praise you Father God. Now prior to being conceived, the Holy Spirit was present handing out divine assignments, and with this assignment, you received a gift or a set of gifts depending on your purpose. Let us not forget everyone has a purpose in his or her lifetime. Some of us will seek out and find our purpose, and there will be others who will wish they would have sought out there purpose in life.

The question is, which one are you? Have you found your purpose? Glory be to God. Now if you are still looking for your purpose, glory be to God because you have not given up on looking for your purpose in life. And if you follow the road map that is presented in this book, I can certainly guarantee that you are headed in the right direction of God opening the doorway of revealing to you his plan for your life.

However, it does require four important things from you in order to receive your purpose from God: repentance, a willing mind, sacrifice, and devoted time.

We will discuss these in a later chapter. However, let's dig right into the heart of receiving anything from God.

First of all, let's get the understanding that everything comes from God, but it comes through the Spirit.

The Spirit, who or what is the spirit? It is a question that we all will ask ourselves at one point in time.

Who is the Spirit? The watcher; the overseer; the protector of the heavenly realm; the heavenly realm transporter deliverer of messages, images, purpose, and assignments brought into the natural realm. The whisperer of instruction and wisdom; that faint, still voice that comes and goes in a gentleman like fashion, not forcing himself to be heard. He's not an intruder but a real friend in your time of need. The one person you can talk to and be real with, and he will always tell you the truth whether you want to hear it or not.

The Spirit is the one who encourages you to push harder beyond your natural ability of fatigue, determination, will, and strength. When you find yourself on the downside of a bad decision from not listening to him, he will bring it to your remembrance. It's going to be okay. He will remind you that your only bad day is the day you have given up on winning in life. You have given up on God. When the doctor says no, it is the spirit that reminds you through your faith, you are healed. It's the spirit that puts your mind at ease when you're confused and struggling with thoughts that don't make sense.

The Spirit is a leader, not a follower. He is the head and not the tail, so you can expect the best from everything you put your hands to do when you allow the Spirit to lead the way.

The Spirt is very strategic at decision-making. Sometimes, you will not like the decisions you will be asked to make, but it will be your choice to listen or not because you don't know the end result of the decision the Spirit is instructing you to enforce. But know this, he will never lie to you or lead you down a path of destruction. The decision you will have to make will be for your best interest and a blessing to others always.

The Spirit does not keep secrets. He shares everything he knows with God. That is why whatever is done in the dark is brought to the light, especially if it is going to bring shame on God. Even when we stray off the path and start feeling ourselves (self-glory), the Spirit will give you a timeline to clean up your mess with his help and instruction. You miss the cleanup due date and your mess is going to get exposed, and you will have to deal with the open shame on your own.

The Spirit is our stop sign from immediate and future harm, always giving us warnings, sometimes sending others in our path to warn us when we are too distracted to listen to him at that moment.

The Spirit is the protector from evil, watching over us even while we sleep at night. That is why it is so important for us to pray before turning in for the night. We not only pray for protection for ourselves, but we pray for everyone especially those in need but do not have a prayer life in place and have no one to intercede on their behalf. Praying for others allows us to receive a peaceful night of sleep because we are doing what the Spirit would want us to do. Pray for others as well as for yourself.

Once you have received your calling from the Spirit, it is hard—nearly impossible—to not want to pray for others, and when you do miss praying, there will be an unction in your own Spirit as though you are missing out on something very important. Believe it or not, it is important that you do it because now the Spirit is holding you accountable for your prayer life. Now, if you miss a night of praying, you will see the conviction of the Spirit reminding you and causing you to be a bit restless until you get it done.

The spirit gives you the strength you will need in your time of need.

That is the whole meaning of praying before you go to bed: prayer of protection for others as well as for yourself from spiritual wickedness while you sleep, as well as the natural wickedness.

My advice to you? Accept the Spirit into your life, invite him into your circle of friends, and let everyone know he is your BFF (best friend forever). Allow him to lead the way in your decision-making always.

Food for thought: I have come to the conclusion that in order for me to achieve all that God has for me to get done, I must keep my circle of friends so small it's even tight for me to get in and out of my own circle.

What is the purpose of the Spirit? The purpose of the Spirit is to aid and assist, to empower and teach you how to use your heavenly gift(s) to do the will of God that you could not have done in your own natural ability. The spirit teaches you how to live a life of sacrifice, accepting God's way of living a righteous life. Enlightenment of your spiritual discernment of truth and righteousness is the Spirit's main objective. Yes, because God despises a liar. I say this because there will be some of you who is going to take grace for granted and use it to be manipulative for your own selfish gain or control of others, and forget this is the residue of the sinful nature residing in the heart that was never given an outdate to allow the Spirit to come in and clean your heart properly but lying in a dormant state, ready to arise when the opportunity presents itself.

Forgetting that God does not look at the outward appearance but reads the inscription in the heart, so I will say it again: God despises a liar and the natural individual of the flesh. A natural man has a tendency of lying and being deceitful sometimes even for no reason, so the Spirit's job is to rid you of the natural desires of corruption and deceitful lusts and teach you to put on the spiritual armor (Eph. 6:11–17, KJV).

Yes, you were chosen by God, and that means you are entitled to receive the heavenly anointment. This entails getting you prepared for the journey ahead, is the main purpose of the Spirit.

Why was I chosen by the Spirit?

Let me rephrase that question. Why were we chosen by the "Spirit"? Simple. God had a plan just for us, and not just a plan for us only but a plan to help his people. That's it, wrapped up in a blanket. God chose us to help his people in this time and season. He didn't choose us because we were prideful, selfish, and disobedient but the complete opposite. God chose us because he could trust us to fulfill his purpose and his plan with his instruction on how to get it done. God chose us because we possessed one distinctive quality that God loves and wants all of his people to get the full understanding of its meaning—love.

We truly have a love for helping people; that's it. Furthermore, we trust solely on him and not ourselves, nor do we allow others to inject their opinions into his plan. If I would have listened to others and disobeyed God, this book would have not been written and I would have never gotten to see what God had in store for me in the next chapter of my life. So to recap on why I was chosen by God, it's because I made my mind up to be obedient to my calling from God. Yes, God knew I was tired of being tired of failure and disappointment. I tried to do everything on my own without his help. God called me and I answered the holy calling.

Being chosen by God to be used as a vessel of honor is the highest honor you will ever receive in this lifetime. However, the cost is high and the lessons are long and can be brutal, but overcoming the challenges are well worth the benefits package that God has set apart for reaching your goal.

When will I know that the Spirit is using me?

There are going to be three gifts the Spirit is going to give you just to let you know he is about to use you. The first gift is your assignment designed specifically just for you, something you will not know how to do in your own natural ability. You will have a strong desire to do something whatever your assignment is. It will actually be calling you day and night, pulling you in that direction. But with your assignment comes opposition, and opposition is about building your character. And you will always have a praise report to give concerning your first gift.

The second gift is preparation time, and you are probably thinking, how is preparation time a gift? God is going to shuffle your life around just like a deck of cards (moving people, places, and things out of the way) and open doors for new opportunities to be presented (time is going to be on your side). Everything going on around you isn't going to matter anymore or affect your grooming time. Your grooming time will be time and space set aside just for you to get started for your future assignment.

Last, but not least, the third gift is peace. You're not going to understand it at first, but you will have a settled state of existence called hope, not knowing where and why it came and you feel the way you feel. These will be the signs to let you know the Spirit is using you. Beyond these gifts, the following seven traits come from the inner you and what you possess in your heart to overcome the challenges to carry the torch of a champion.

A WILLING MIND

A willing mindset has obtained a fixed state of being obedient. This next question is going to require some thinking on your part.

How can I get a willing mind? Let me give you about fifteen seconds just to ponder on the question. Okay, time is up. A willing mind has a two-step process that needs your full attention, and it does require a little work on your part.

Food for thought: Nothing in life is worth having if you don't put in the time and work to obtain it.

Now, the first step of acquiring a willing mind is to gain the full understanding and the acceptance of the principle of repentance.

Principle of repentance: submissively humbling yourself to ask God for forgiveness for your sins and to help you to forgive those who have sinned against you.

The key element of repentance is admittance and willingness to shine a light on your thoughts and actions. Repenting conforms you to hold yourself accountable for your bad behavior, and willingly turning away from such behavior while also admitting that your thinking was wrong and you do need help and guidance.

It is not embarrassing to admit that you need help and guidance.

I must admit there was a time in my own life when I did not care about the mistakes I was making–young and dumb—when I lived life on the edge of trial and error. Trying to fit in the wrong crowd. Just getting into all types of shenanigans, I will learn as I go, if it does not kill me. I won't do that again.

Yes, that was my thinking, and my negative behavior pattern did align with my negative thoughts, giving me an unwilling mindset to obedience.

But now, I can thank God because he had a plan for me, and his plan was better than anything I could have put together for myself. But it required me to put in some work and let go of myself and give my way of thinking and living over to God. Getting out of my own way was one-third of the battle. But God had to have my undivided attention, so getting away from my old environment and everyone that aligned with that old mindset was needed. I was determined to see a change in my life. I was determined to get it right this time, find my gift, and use it wisely.

Most of the time, we can be lightning fast to ask to be forgiven, but we tend to go back to our old ways and habits if we don't learn to forgive ourselves.

Food for thought: Learning to forgive yourself is learning to love yourself

Sometimes, we tend to get amnesia when it's time to forgive others' actions against us. Because we feel betrayed and deep down we want just a little revenge—not a whole lot, just enough to let the person or people who have wronged us know they didn't get away with nothing and we are even.

Believe it or not, we all have felt this undesirable way of thinking at one point in time or another, and this is a selfish way of thinking.

This act of thinking has a name, and I call it selfish revenge. It comes from the actions of someone who has felt the pain or humiliation of hurt.

Self-destructive thinking at its worst is when you want to inflict pain or humiliation on someone in a vengeful mindset. Letting go and letting God handle that situation is sometimes a hard thing to do because we tend to think that God moves too slow for us and we want instant revenge while the pain of hurt is fresh. This is that mindset that prevents prayers from being heard and getting answered.

Vengeance is mine: "I will repay," saith the Lord (Romans 12:19 KJV).

Now, the willing mind is a sound but reasoning mindset: determined to gather useful information, diligent toward wise counsel, and shunning all aspects of wrong doings and the presence of evil. Yes, focused in the pursuit of achieving peace. Yes, I said *peace*, and you are probably wondering why I would say peace and not the pursuit of the temporal facets of life (fame, riches, power, or possibly happiness). It is because all of these can be here today and gone tomorrow. Whereas peace is not manmade or derived from your selfish ambitions. The gift of peace comes solely from God with no strings attached. The gift of peace is one of the most treasured gifts you could ever receive because it's completely yours and it's totally earned by you through obedience.

The mission of the willing mind is to help you achieve something more gratifying than material possessions through your own natural ability.

The willing mind has a goal, and this entails living a life of peace and being a blessing to others.

Question: how can I be a blessing to others if I am not blessed?

Simple—you can't. But there is someone who can give you the resources and the means to be a blessing to others, and he's not expecting nothing in return. However, to acquire these resources from God, it is a requirement that I must have a willing mindset and peace in my own life in order to be a blessing to someone else and not expect nothing in return. You have probably heard the old clichés that some people will use from time to time. You have probably experienced the end result or probably were the perpetrators of these actions.

"I am not going to do nothing for someone who will not do something for me," "If I do this for you, now you owe me a favor"—these are selfish people doing what they do, performing selfish acts for their own selfish gain. It's okay to be a blessing to others and not expecting nothing in return. This is one of the kindest gestures of doing for others as you would want done to you. This is that simple road map leading to the path of peace and once you find peace, you will find out this is true happiness.

It's okay to be happy.

However, we don't live in a perfect world and most of us will find one or the other: blessing without the real happiness or the fake happiness without the blessing. Whatever the case may be for you, know this—it is possible to have both blessing and real happiness, which is really called peace.

Let's take a break for about two minutes and think about peace. Now examine your own life. Now, this is that time in your life when you have to be truthful to yourself this is between you and God.

Now answer these two questions truthfully: (1) Do I have peace in my life? (2) Am I at peace with myself?

If your answer was yes to both questions, then you are in a blessed state in your life at this present season. Glory be to God, and I would like to recommend that you continue your present journey. Now if you answered no to either one of those questions, I am compelled to slow down just for you so that you can receive the understanding of how to have peace in your life and be at peace with yourself.

Right now, you are probably saying, "I know how to have peace in my life—mind my own business and stay in the house" or "mind my own business and keep people out of my business and only deal with those people who won't cause friction." Temporary solution for a life-long answer. This is not happening if you truly want to live a life of peace. Following these three simple instructions will help put you on the path of getting real happiness—peace—to reside with you.

Either you are going to get it or you are not going to get it.

The road map to peace. This next set of instructions will be like the GPS in your vehicle. Try this for seven days: beginning individuals (five minutes each set of instructions for seven days); mature individuals (ten minutes each set of instructions for seven days); and prayer warriors (fifteen minutes each set of instructions for seven days).

1. Rise and shine sleepy head. You are now entering the prayer zone. You will need to get up each morning before the crack of dawn between the time of 3am-7am. Find a designated space or room in your home, and for five min-

utes, spend some quiet time with God. First of all, I want you to give God his praise report. Acknowledge or thank God for allowing you to come into his presence. Thank him for who he is. And thank him for this day that you are presently presenting yourself in his presence to ask for forgiveness of all your sins—past, present, and future. Pray for yourself. Pray for your peace, pray for healing, pray for your deliverance (adultery, alcohol, drugs, fornication, sexual perversion). Pray for your light to shine in this dark world. Learning to pray for yourself—nothing else. Leave everything else out of your prayer for yourself.

2. Now for five minutes, pray for guidance. Pray for your ears to be opened that you may hear the voices of truth. Pray for your heart to be cleansed so that you can hear the voice of the Holy Spirit. Pray for your mind to be open to new ideas, pray for your eyes to see the path that you are traveling on, pray for you getting out of your own way and let God lead the way, and pray to ask God to take a little bit out of his time to talk to you just so you know he is there with you. Remember, leave everything else out of your prayer for guidance.

3. Now for the last five minutes, pray for other people. Yes, pray for those who have done you wrong or despitefully tried to use you, pray for those who have not found the path of righteousness, pray for the ones that are destined to come across your path as a seed planter. Pray for the ones who come to water the seed, and we know God will give the increase. Learning to pray just for others is the lesson.

Food for thought: You can never truly find peace if you are living a lie.

As you continue to read, don't wait to the end of the book to do the above exercise. Do it immediately while you are still reading so that everything is fresh and you're getting the full understanding of the lesson.

Now, whichever level you partake to complete is solely upon you learning to seek. Ask and receive the gift of peace. The gift of peace only comes to those who choose to have a willing mind of obedience, and being obedient starts with following simple instructions.

The second step of the willing mind process is learning to sacrifice.

I say this with sadness on my heart: not everyone is willing to do what it takes to get peace in their own life. It's really hard to imagine just living your entire life in commotion and confusion, torn between living for God and living for the world.

Can you imagine walking around all day long with a migraine headache and no pills to help relieve the pain? This is what you can expect trying to live life on both sides of the fence—no peace and forced to live in confusion until you make a life-changing decision. There will be some of you who would rather sit back idle, criticize, and complain about how life is so hard and unfair, blaming others for your shortcomings and using the lame excuse, "I am just going to wait on the Lord. And if he gives it to me, then it's meant for me to have it, but if he does not, then it wasn't meant."

Wake up and stop dreaming. Stop living life wishing for what was already meant for you to have and do what's expected of you to get it. Don't just stand by watching others living and enjoying a life of peace, failing to see that you too could be living a life of peace. But instead, you insist on compromising, doing absolutely nothing or just enough to get by while still complaining. I call this routine living: scared of your own shadow, afraid of your own potential, terrified to walk out of your comfort zone. That's right, living life in your own little bubble, not enjoying life to its fullest, no outside communication or relationships, and especially no peace.

Wow, in my own personal experience, I have met quite a few people on this journey especially while writing this book. They were afraid of the challenge to do better because of the possibility of missing the mark—a fear of failure. Living their life wondering about what others would think and say about their failed attempts, so instead of self-inflicted embarrassment, they insist on not trying at all.

Food for thought: Fear is the enemy to peace, and you could never learn to apply the two-step process of a willing mind while living in fear.

Answer this one question: Would you be willing to sacrifice all of the worldly pleasures of a sinful life for your peace?

If you are undecided with the answer to this question, that means you are not ready to live a life of peace. In order to obtain and maintain peace in your life, you must be willing to sacrifice all things in life.

Starting with yourself, family, friends, time, and money—all for the love for God. Sacrifice pushes you to look beyond your flaws and imperfections, allowing your mind to maximize on your strengths and overcome your weaknesses with undistorted (sound) thinking.

Let's take a closer look at an example. For instance, a battery runs on a positive and negative charge intake, which in turn produces the necessary energy needed for a positive result. That is the same with sacrifice. I am willing to let go of my negative thinking and bad habits knowing that it's wrong and leading me down the path of failure and destruction. I refuse to lie to myself; there will be some consequences for my actions if I continue down the wrong path. However, I am willing to sacrifice all the negativity that I hold on to for a more fulfilling reward of walking in love and peace, letting go of all the negative people and activity altogether to walk the path of my destiny. This in turn produces a willing mindset headed in the direction of obtaining peace.

Sacrificing is not easy. There will be a lot of division in your life due to you making a stand to sacrifice for your destiny. Believe it or not, it's going to start in your own household and then extended family and friends.

It's hard to imagine being torn between God and family because we were taught that family is all we got and blood is thicker than water. You will find it hard to comprehend that there will be family members who don't want to see you trying to live life serving God and living in peace.

But be encouraged and ask God to help you with living in sacrifice because sacrifice isn't something you can turn on and off like a light switch. Once it's turned on, it must stay on for a lifetime. Now, that's the hardest part of sacrificing: most people cannot handle the fact of being cut off from social (family) gatherings, which involves all the attributes of the old life they have been delivered from because they choose to live for God and they want to be accepted at the social gatherings.

Stop it right now and get over it. You are cut off from the world's way of living because God has something better for you. Sacrificing keeps all aspects of life in its proper order. My past life is my past, and I cannot live in the present with my past dictating my future.

There will always be people who will want to shine the light on your past, who wants nothing more than to never let you forget about your past. It's like a broken record whenever you see them or talk with them. They are always singing that same sad old song only to remind you of the past and who keeps a broken record on the shelf. So shame on them and their behavior. Cut them off, pray for them, and keep it moving—in that order, plain and simple.

You can't be afraid to move on. You are being held accountable for your own destiny if they can't celebrate with you on being delivered from the past. Oh well, your relationship with God is more rewarding in the long run anyway. God has a way of clearing your path, and it's up to you to keep it cleared.

Once the path is clear, this is your sign from God that he has appointed this time for you to get prepared to walk the path of your destiny, and for name's sake, I call it devoted time. Spending time with you and God only. You will have to manage your devoted time very wisely. Remember, life is still going on all around you. And once again, sacrificing everything for your quiet time is imperative. It's your training time. You spending time talking with and listening to instructions from God has to have devotion in that Kool-Aid.

Remember, beware of those wolves in sheep's clothing. They really don't want to see you in a willing mindset. They really feel as though you don't deserve a new beginning. You will know them by their fruit.

Pray for them and keep it moving.

Why is it that guilt and condemnation always seem to come knocking when God is doing something?

The presence of evil will never let up until it uproots all the good that God has created, so be mindful and watchful of all the tricks of the enemy.

It will be hard for some individuals to comprehend the possibility that the willing mindset did not come from a classroom environment. It came only through obedience to God. A willing mind can take you places a formal education cannot go, and I am not saying a formal education is not good to have under your belt. It is a plus if you desire to work and live by the world's standard of living. But God has shown me that I don't need a formal education to bear fruit in the kingdom. God has a plan for his chosen, and it all starts with a willing mind. As one of his chosen champions, I have a mission in this life. And that is to help others gain the knowledge of being obedient, obtain the Spirit of peace, and learn how to carry the torch of God's chosen champion for the next generation to come.

Food for thought: The steps of the righteous are ordered by the Lord, and they are called to produce fruit for the next generation.

BELIEVE IN YOURSELF

News flash: if I were to do a survey with three people and ask them the question about the title of this chapter, believe me. I can most definitely assume that I would hear three different ways of self-exploitation. However, this chapter is not headed in the direction of self-exploitation but to teach you to believe in something, by far, much greater than yourself.

Before you start to lay judgement on the last statement I made, I want you to please refrain your thoughts from going into a negative mindset but to sit back and be open-minded just for a moment. Yes, I asked the question, do you believe in yourself? Before I give my answer to this question, I will say everyone in their right mind would say, "Yes, I believe in myself because if I don't believe who will, and what can I accomplish if I don't believe in me?" Well, guess what? Life is bigger than you or me, and the world does not revolve around us and our feelings. I had to learn this tough lesson the hard way before I was entrusted to write this book.

Food for thought: I trust God, I believe in Jesus, I have faith in the Holy Spirit.

Well, let's dig right into the subject matter. I am going to disagree; I don't believe in myself anymore. Most people would think that believing in yourself is a sign of strength and becoming successful would shortly follow. Now on the flipside of the coin, most people would look down on others as a sign of weakness for not believing in themselves and consider this as a main factor as to why they wouldn't push themselves in striving to have or to do better in life.

I must admit that I was guilty of having a self-righteous attitude, a haughty and prideful spirit, arrogant to the point of self-destruction, looking down on people that I knew I was doing just a little bit better than them. And this mindset caused me to prolong my gift of writing and receiving my blessing, which entailed knowing my mission in life.

I not only prolonged what was meant for me to have, but I made more enemies than friends even within my own family. I only thought about myself and my gain. That is why it would be a terrible mistake on my behalf to settle for anything less than believing in the greater good. "Life is bigger than me and God had to open my eyes to the truth before he could use me as a vessel for his glory."

As a younger adult, I made a lot of bad choices because I chose to believe in me and my way of doing things. And because of my hard head and unwillingness to listen to anyone or take any advice, pride, arrogance, and know-it-all attitude settled in, and I found myself always crashing head first at the end of a dead-end street that I put myself on.

But God, knowing how hardheaded I was, kept me safe and allowed me to gain a lot of personal experience or personal wisdom. He knew back then that one day, I would get it right and I would get the understanding from the lessons of life. I would be writing books teaching on his mercy and goodness, giving him all the glory. However, in order for me to get on the right track, he allowed me to hit rock bottom, and while I sat there in self-pity, I began praying and asking God why was my life in such a mess.

He revealed it to me by showing me a flashback of my life and all the years of my running around in circles like a puppy chasing his tail looking for the Scooby snack. He showed me that everything I was doing was only for myself, and I wasn't about to share my Scooby snack with anyone or help anybody else because in my mind, I felt as though I did it on my own and I was going to pay myself by myself.

Self-made in my mind, I created my own glory, I walked in my own light, and I did not have to answer to no one. Sad but true, I was so broken on the inside because of the path that I was on, and I could not see how to get off of it. I didn't see a future for myself or a light of hope to come back and regain my identity. Even today, every now and then, I find myself riding down the street, pulling over just to have a good cry and a moment of silence just to thank God for delivering me and giving me real hope again.

Back then, I asked God to help me, and I told him that if he revealed himself to me and showed me that I wasn't alone, I would be a soldier in his army for life. Even now, sometimes I find myself in difficult decisions because of my love for God and family. His grace is sufficient in all of the choices that I make when it comes to dealing with family that don't know God and those who know him but not really trying to live for him. So it all boils down to me making a choice between what is right and wrong in God's eyes. Furthermore, I don't want his grace to run out on me from my choices on how to deal with my family.

Food for thought: I love God and I love family, but I love God more.

Right now, before we go any further, let's get an understanding. God knows us better than we know ourselves, so he challenged me to hold true to the promise that I made to him if he revealed himself to me. Now that wasn't the hard part. But getting me to believe (that was the key—getting me to believe) was what he needed to do in order for me to accept and acknowledge who he was and serve in the kingdom for a lifetime.

That's one thing I personally know about God. He has a way of getting our attention. And I thank him for his leniency because as hardheaded as I was, he didn't have to do anything drastic to get my attention (strip me of my health or a life-changing issue). He did something amazing, and he knew I would be in awe and ready to listen.

So God sent an angel to me—yes, an angel. Now I will admit it, though I wouldn't be talking about it right now if God had not told me to write about it. Even though it might sound spooky to some, there are others who are reading this book and have experienced this. They know what I am talking about but have not openly mentioned it because of fear and disbelief. I feel you and I share your thoughts. But on the other hand, yes, this is that secret that I held in my heart that has kept me grounded in keeping my personal relationship with God intact.

I have accepted the inquiring minds of family and friends who have questioned why I live for God and why I gave up on chasing after the Scooby snacks. My testimony is real, and now you all get to hear my testimony and why I made the decision to separate myself from my past completely.

The angel that was sent told me that my prayers were heard and he was here visiting me on behalf of the promise I made to God. The angel told me that I was very hardheaded, and he had to show me something in order to convince me that God was real and he has and always is watching over me. On three separate occasions in our five-minute conversation, he instructed me to close my eyes and open them, and each time I closed and opened my eyes, there appeared evil spirits. These were the spirits that walked around infracting the lives of unbelievers.

But this one night, I was given the ability to look inside the spiritual realm and see what God wanted me to see in order to show me that he was real, I was being protected for a purpose bigger than myself, and he would always be with me. Now, after the third round, the angel told me, "You are so hardheaded." But I was convinced, and from that evening, my life did change. I made a promise that I couldn't afford to break, and that was to be a soldier in God's army for life.

I've broken a lot of promises early on in my life, and I have seen the after effects of those broken promises. But this was one I couldn't imagine what the end result would be if I didn't at least try to keep it. So here I am today, being that soldier. Now, the part I failed to mention was that I was fully awake—not sleeping but awake.

So my testimony of God revealing himself to me was enough for me to gain the understanding: I cannot believe in myself when there is a God ruling the heavenly and natural realm in whole supremacy.

Food for thought: Practice is the key to perfection, and perfection is the key to practice.

The food for thought exemplifies an individual with a talent and is willing to diligently practice hard and receive the necessary training to get better at their talent. These individuals are willing to accept the challenge to excel above their peers. They don't just sit back and believe in themselves. No, they believe in their talent, or else they won't push themselves to train harder to be better than their peers. They push themselves beyond their own expectations. (To be the best, you must work harder than the rest.) Their level of confidence propels them to believe in their talent and not just themselves.

I am saying that believing in yourself is a wrong mindset to have. It forces you to think more of yourself than what you really are. This is a harmful mindset (putting yourself on a pedestal) that will always cause you to stumble every time. Now being confident is something else. It's a thin line between love and hate, and it's even thinner with believing in yourself and confidence in yourself. We will touch on that just a little later.

Stinking thinking is what I would call it when you allow yourself to think more of yourself than you should; you have now started smelling yourself—stinking thinking—smelling your own nasty thoughts.

God said it in his word: "I am a jealous God." You will not love anything or anyone more than you love me.

The food for thought advice instructs you to think outside the box and work on building your personal relationship with God in which he is a rewarder of those who diligently seek after him.

Spending quality time with God is required in order to maintain a personal relationship with God. I cannot say I have a personal relationship with God if I don't take time out of my so-called busy schedule and spend time in reading God's word. Walking and talking with God; patiently waiting to hear from God; being obedient to whatever he has me to do; thanking God for what he has already done for me; and praising God in my daily time (throughout the day, recognizing and thanking him)—building on my relationship with him is building my house on a solid foundation (rock) to God.

This does not include your thinking of believing in yourself. When you started believing in yourself, you also started loving yourself more than anything else. Gradually, everything about you start to change.

Food for thought: Selfishness and pride are the cousins of self-destruction.

Now, if you are in disagreement about what I am saying, I did ask you to refrain from negative thoughts and be open-minded while reading this chapter. Now, I am going to ask you to challenge what I am saying and ask someone who is really close to you, someone who is always around you or has been around for a while.

Am I selfish? Am I prideful?

The truth will not kill you, but it will get you to examine your behavior just a little bit closer.

Remember the people that love you will certainly be truthful, but there are ones who side with you and know you are a mess but don't want to tell you because they might be afraid of losing their personal gain. You will see that your circle of associates will get smaller if you are willing to examine and admit the truth to yourself. If you don't already know, know this fact: everyone wants to be on a winning team, even if they have to be deceitful, by not biting the hand that puts money in their pockets.

I would have never thought I would have gained some haters, but it's better to know who they are so I can stay away, than allow them to be in my presence and talk about me behind my back.

You will have some haters, but guess what? Even the haters want to be affiliated with a winner, hoping to see you fall and eventually ask them for something so that they can get the pleasure of saying no and be able to talk about your down fall to others. This is their own personal gain. You will know the haters: they are the ones who will celebrate with you secretly but always have an excuse not to celebrate with you publicly because they have put their mouth on you in secret. So those are not truthful opinions. It's the ones who has nothing to gain from you but love to see you living your best life.

Confidence

Confidence on the other hand is something totally different. It gives you the inner drive to strive for something you may think is important to you at that moment. Confidence is a feeling that comes and goes like the wind, an adrenaline rush that can be turned on and off whenever it's needed.

But guess what? We shouldn't live our lives based around our emotions and our feelings, but the truth of the matter is most of us do just that. We live our lives based on how we feel about certain situations and how we feel about certain people.

As your relationship grows with God, he teaches you how to live your life based around truth and love. How can I tell you that I love you when I do not understand the meaning of love or I have not displayed knowing how to love myself first? Everyone wants to be loved even if they haven't learned how to give love in return, and that's the same with the truth.

No one likes to be lied to or lied on. So we align ourselves up with people whom we think will accommodate these two factors, truth and love, in our life. Most of the time, we fall short because we tend to lose focus by believing in people and casting a shadow over God and his love for us until we need to ask him for something. I will say this confidence is a good thing to have because it belongs to you and it is your choice to use it whenever you need it.

It is not designed to hurt nor tear anyone down. It's specifically made for the purpose of building your character and establishing that inner drive within you.

Food for thought: You can never have too much confidence, but you can be a slowpoke without enough of it.

This is that thinner line that I mentioned earlier in the chapter.

I am confident in myself because he that lives in me is greater than he that lives in the world. I can do whatever it is God has planned for me to accomplish because now I know that it was God who gave me a reason to hope.

I am confident in my faith. Faith without works is dead. The gift that God instructed to me to use is not just for me but for the world to see how God can transform the life of a sinner and give me untainted belief.

I am confident in the love that I am willing to show to others, not expecting the same love in return. However, God showed me there is no love greater than his love for me.

I am confident in trust. However, God showed me how to put my trust in him and not in people.

I am confident this gift of writing is from God, and I will use it to exhort and uplift God's word and magnify his name above all that I do and teach others about God's love for his people.

My confidence in my relationship with God is what keeps me grounded and focused on living for God. Now, as one of his chosen champions for this era, I encourage you to diligently seek after God for your assignment in life before it's too late and you miss out on living your best life.

STUBBORN TO DEFEAT
(PRAYER LIFE)

We are in the fourth quarter in the seventh game of the finals, down by two points with thirty seconds on the clock. You call time-out and the previous play. Before the time-out, your best man fell and hurt his knee and his shooting hand. Now you as the coach, you have a life-changing decision to make within three choices.

1. Your best man is pleading with you to stay in the game, willing to tough it out. "Coach, it's the last game of the finals. Don't take me out. We have made it this far. I can go thirty seconds." As he pleads his case, you are analyzing the risk of worsening the injury, possibly losing him for half of next season because of the severity of his injury. What do you do as the coach?

2. You have a man on the bench who has not played during the finals. He is one of your go-to players in a crunch play. However, his conduct of partying and being late to practices and displaying a lack of moral support for the team is the reason why he hasn't played. During the regular season, he has come through with some spectacular plays, getting to the free throw line, hitting the big shot at the buzzer. What do you do as the coach?

3. You take your last time-out (go and pray) and buy a little time for your best man to muster up every bit of endurance in him because in the back of your mind, you know you need him in the game win or lose.

But are you willing to have management frown on your decision of keeping him in the game if you lose? However, the game plan is to have him on the floor even in pain to be a slight distraction to the defense and go for a Hail Mary with your bench guy. Call the play for him to drive to the rim and draw the foul he has a high percentage in made free throws. Make the decision, Coach.

An individual goes to the doctor, and the doctor gives him a bad health report. He also tells the individual he might want to get his business affairs in order because he only has three months to live. You could not even imagine what would be going on inside this individual's mind if you have not walked in those shoes. However, it is a life-changing decision that must be made at this time. You've got three choices.

1. Go get a second opinion and hope the first doctor was mistaken. If both opinions are the same, now you will have to be at peace with the results and have some fun till the end.
2. Throw in the towel, go get drunk, and commit suicide. Now this is the enemy at work in full force to distract you from hope and take you out.
3. Listen to what the two doctors have stated and do not receive that in your spirit. Now go get in your prayer closet and call on the best healer the world has ever known.

The doctors have given up and said no, but God can override with a yes if you call him. You will have to be willing to give up everything pertaining to this worldly living in order to get the healing you are asking for. Remember, God knows your heart and your actions, so the trade is a life-changing decision, and the trade for your health is a promise you must keep before God and people. So you must come in truth and believe that he can and will heal you. Now you decide.

A couple is married for more than twenty years. They wake up one day and decided it was time for a divorce—not a separation but a divorce. Failing to recall their marriage vows, they have made an emotional decision to part ways. Forgetting only through death do they part; and they promise to love each other through the good and the bad, through sickness and health, through rich and poor. If you have been married and now you are divorced, you pretty much have a handle on this situation. But let's take a closer look, and you decide what could have been an alternate outcome besides getting divorced. You have three choices.

Now this is a life-changing decision that will affect everyone in the family.

1. There was infidelity, lack of financial support, verbal and physical abuse, drugs and alcohol issues, but you stayed around ten more years while all this was going on in the first ten years. However, you never considered seeking counsel to save the marriage. Instead, you chose to bail out without a resolution.

Food for thought: Hasty decision-making will always leave room for regret later.

2. Marriage is like a roller coaster. It goes up and down, and bends and twists around the curves of life at a high rate of speed, causing everyone to scream and rethink if they will ever get on this ride again. The roller coaster even goes through loops, and everyone holds on for dear life with the hope of staying on till the ride stops. Divorce gives us an outlet when the ride stops. So now in the back of your mind, you have an option to just go through the motions of marriage and bail out with a divorce when you think a better opportunity has presented itself.

Food for thought: Shame on you thinking the grass is greener on the other side.

3. We came into this marriage in agreement. Now let's work on a solution in agreement. We will do something totally

different. Let's go to God together, putting everything on the altar. It's between you and God, but we are in agreement to do it together.

Keep God first and he will keep you married.

You have just read three examples of life-changing decisions in which there are many more we could address. However, this book is not big enough to go through everything specifically, but it is designed to get you to look at issues you will encounter in life with three possible solutions. But the best answer for each issue above, and your own that you will incur, will be to pray first including, God in all of your life-changing decisions.

Food for thought: Every coin has two sides, but a third outlook is in place (heads, tails, and the flip), not knowing where it's going to land.

Prayer life is the key element to living your best life. We all have known or might have heard of someone who was doing very well in life, career, and finances, but due to unknown circumstances, they lived a very sad life behind closed doors. They invested all of their time and energy into a temporary lifestyle, thinking that the good times will never end. But—and it's always that but—when you compromise with the worldly way of living, the good times do come to an end and now you have missed out on the best investment.

Prayer life investment

Prayer life is the best invested time you can count on in the long run. This is time that cannot be taken away or never get old. Prayer life will be with you forever even when everyone and everything around you has moved on and slowed down completely. Your prayer life is the only thing in this life that you can truly count on and get a definitive return on your invested time you put in. Your prayer life will reflect exactly what you put into it. You can only withdraw what you've deposited or accumulated through time-vested gain.

GOD LOVES A CHAMPION

I can live a fake life and make my mouth say anything in front of the spectators, and live a sad life behind closed doors. And when the time comes, I need a prayer to get heard and answered in my time of need. Now that mouth is singing a different tune, begging and pleading for God to hear me and for others to pray for my situation when they don't even pray for themselves.

Food for thought: Life has a boot for you when the well is dry in your prayer life.

Let's get a clear understanding. You are responsible for your own prayer life. Just like you are responsible to pay your own bills and to keep up with your own personal hygiene. You, you, you—it's you who is responsible to make sure your prayers are getting heard. It's you who has the responsibility to make time and spend quality time with God. He is the same God you will be asking others to pray to for your situation when it's your responsibility to build your own personal relationship with him.

You will not need to ask anyone to pray on your behalf because you don't think you can get a prayer through. God loves us all, but it is up to you to build on that love by spending time with him just like you would do if you encountered a situation that you know only he could pull you through it. God knows who is coming in truth, so when you come to him, be real even if you are coming to ask for something. Just for that moment, keep it real.

Remember this, God knows how to get your attention any time he wants it, but he wants us to use that free will that he has given us. And when you only come because you want something, he's not offended because he is a loving and forgiving God, plus he is in the blessing business.

Does God give out selfish blessings? I don't think so. Selfishness means you only want it for your glory and yourself, and I don't see where yours includes God in it at all. So I know God looks at this as well. Why would he answer a prayer for you and you take all the credit for yourself? No way, homey. Don't play like that. God knows the factors behind every prayer he is going to answer. You come faking it, you don't want to spend time trying to get to know him. You're trying to use his kindness and grace for your own personal gain.

You will be waiting a long time to get a prayer answered. I am not saying he is not listening, but getting him to move on your request is the result of what he has thought about your situation before you even came to him about it. I will say this out of love: don't wait until you need something from God before you come to him in prayer.

Take a break from your busy schedule and spend some time with him just to say hi or ask how his day is. I am sure he will appreciate the thought of you thinking about him and asking about his well-being. You just might get to hear from him asking you the same thing, and hopefully you will be able to answer. "Father God, I am doing okay, thanks to you." Let him know you are acknowledging him for who he is, and appreciating all that he has done for you and is going to do for you, not just for what you want anytime you feel the urge to selfishly request to get a prayer answered.

I don't like to elaborate on others' personal requests, so I am going to use myself as an example in this case. When I need something, I call my Father God. When I am unsure about a situation, I sit myself down and I talk to my Father God. It's really hard for me to call anyone outside of God to look for answers when everyone else is looking for answers or in need of help for their own situations. But most of us are looking for answers in all the wrong places. I stay in my own lane; I keep God first and he is keeping me. I can only advise you to follow the road map that has guided me down the path that I am on by allowing the GPS of God, which is the Holy Spirit, give you the directions that God has intended for you to receive so that you may achieve all that God has planned for you. I can tell you this: I can't do nothing without God. I want his approval in everything that I do.

Food for thought: Who is your best friend forever? Mine is God.

I am going to be a little transparent in this chapter. I have been on the short end of the stick most of my life, always looking for an

outlet to get ahead but always falling short. I never received the support that you would think you could get from striving to get ahead
in life, so I made my mind up to live for God with no options of
divorce. Since then, I have watched my life move in the direction
that I know it's all God and not my doing.

I share this with you because there is someone who's reading
this book right now who needs to hear this and know that my story
is not just my own but their story as well. Our stories were not at all
peaches and cream. I have been tried through the fire, and God was
and has always been there with me. I am watching him do it now
through this book.

I made up my mind that I was tired of losing, and when this life
was over, I didn't want to go to hell. Just the thought of going to hell
is too scary for me to want to be there. I don't have any associates that
I would want to be in hell with suffering for a lifetime, so I might as
well get on the winning side of life and join the winning team. God
has never lost, so why wouldn't I want to join up with a winning
team? I don't have to worry about sitting the bench or being cut from
the team. It's all up to me. Through God, I cannot lose. Through
God, I cannot quit. Through God, I am a winner.

As you walk your journey, you are going to encounter three
types of people: those who want to see you successful, those who
don't, and those who are there to help you get to where you are going.
Those who want to see you succeed are the ones who don't have to
deal with you while you are trying to get to where you going. Those
who don't care are the ones who would rather not see you make it just
so they can have something to talk about for years to come. Those
who are there to help were meant to be there just when the time is
right for you to deal with them.

Food for thought: They smile in your face while stabbing you
in the back.

You are going to have people saying all types of negative remarks
to try and get you off track, but this is your lesson to learn on how

to stay focused. If you fail this lesson, you will definitely have to redo the lesson and retake the test again and again till you pass.

You are going to deal with deceptive people (lying spirits) on all levels. Once again, it's only a lesson that you must learn and pass the test with flying colors. The lesson is going to teach you to pay attention to your surroundings and the people you allow to be in your presence. If people can see you don't value your time and money, they are going to lie and steal (borrow with no intentions of paying you back) every chance they can get.

God has unlimited resources, and his people are placed in all walks of life. Just his saying yes opens all of his resources geared to you for what he has planned on your behalf.

God chose you just like he had chosen little David, whose final destiny was to be King David. Little David as a young lad was predestined by God to be one of God's chosen champions. Later crowned as king of God's people, he began his journey early on in life. Learning the art of war with the simplicity of available tools to his disposal, a slingshot, King David displayed the traits of a champion through the defeat of the giant Goliath.

Some would seem to think that David as a young lad was prideful, a little arrogant, and stubborn, but he had the one key ingredient that God loved about him above all things. He had a love for God. David would sing to God and write songs about God. He would praise and preach about God. No doubt, his love for God was always on display, and confessing God before man was his ultimate sacrifice. If Goliath were still around today, he too would also tell you about David's confession of doing battle in the name of the Lord.

I want to encourage you to follow the path of your destiny. Give the Holy Spirit permission over your life. Allow the Holy Spirit to teach you and guide you onto your destiny as one of God's chosen champions. Nothing is impossible for our God. If you were chosen to be a champion, that means God knew you could handle the position. God has never lost a battle. Let us join forces with him as labor champions for the kingdom of heaven. God is a rewarder of those who stand up in honor of him receiving glory. Join me as we join the battle for the salvation of souls on God's behalf as one of his esteemed champions.

The world is not going to accept us. But I say, "Okay," because I come in the name of the Lord and you will have to deal with me.

The world is not going to like us or celebrate with us. But I say, "Okay." As long as we have God on our side, we will be okay.

The host of family and friends are going to walk away. But I say, "Okay." We were never that tight anyway.

The world is going to talk about us behind our back. But I say, "Okay," because it's none of our business what they say anyway.

In closing, we all have been through some rough patches in this life.

Never give in, never give up. I have found my gift and my purpose in this life. My calling from God has pushed me forward to enlighten God's chosen to get off the couch and do something. Open your eyes to the opportunities that God has presented before you.

It's okay to say yes to God and no to the world. It only sounds the alarm that there are new champions on the way.

We are stubborn to defeat.

WORK HARDER

There is an old cliché that we used back in the day in reference to the title of this chapter—work smarter, not harder. But in the real world, working harder pays off and brings aboard the greater reward. However, this chapter is not in rebuttal of working smarter but encourages you to work harder in maintaining your spiritual life.

Let's take a quick look at some everyday living. You get up in the morning, get yourself cleaned up and dressed, have a little breakfast, get your lunch together for work, and now you're off to start the day to make money so that you can take care of yourself and your loved ones. Okay, we get that now. This becomes a normal day from Monday to Friday and possibly some weekends for overtime. We all have done this to the point of retirement or quitting to find something better that is less work but equal to or more than the amount of pay we were getting.

This is the American dream—to make more money without having to work harder unless we are doing something we really like doing so it doesn't feel like work. In reality, this is what we all must do in order to maintain our materialistic lifestyle and showboating, like we have it really going on. Okay, I get it. But what about your spiritual life? This is the other side of life that is taken for granted, and most people only think about it when they fall on hard times. And when things turn around and life looks like it's back on track again, they forget about their spiritual life until they need it again.

Some will look at the spiritual life as if it's like going to the doctor if they feel an ailment or in need of a checkup—"I better make an appointment to see my doctor." And this is the same mindset when the natural side of life is going haywire. Oh, let me call on God to help me through this issue so I can have me a testimony to share with others in case I need to ask them for a helping hand. This is the mindset of most people who only look at getting over or try to use others for their own selfish benefit. You will have people actually working harder in trying to be deceitful when they can just keep it real and wait on the power of God to manifest itself into their own lives.

Believe it or not, your spiritual life is more important than your natural life. Falling on hard times is just an easier way to learn this lesson, reveal to you the real from the fake, and who's got your back when you really need some help or need to get a prayer answered.

Like always, I will use myself as an example. You and I are best of associates, occasional weekend happy-hour drinks, and once a month bar hopping, looking for the gullible lonely chick for a quick one-night stand just to have a laugh at work. We get the news they are cutting back on personnel. I get laid off, and that same associate who was okay with me when I had a job is no longer taking my phone calls and is actually doing everything in their power to avoid me. No longer an occasional associate but a never-knew-you stranger now that hard times have intruded in on my life, I am back to square one, praying to God for some help and disappointed from the lack of compassion from losing my job. This example is a scenario that goes on and on in everyone's life at one time or another, or different issues that will arise from our poor decisions. We learn to fall back on God.

Some will use God as a safety net—let me live my life my way, and when I need help, I will call on God. Some will use God as Santa Claus—give me what I want and I might keep praying. Some will say there is no God and I am my own god, but they look to those who love and worship God to help them in any of their crises that they might encounter. But I am here to tell you how important it is to work harder on the most important relationship you will ever obtain in this life, and that is your relationship with God.

If you are the gospel music lover that I have grown to become, I would like to recommend you to listen to a song by Donald Lawrence and The Tri-City Singers, featuring Dewayne Woods, "God Is." Yes, God is my everything. And when I say this, I mean it with all my heart. I cannot do nothing without talking with God about it or asking his permission. I need to have God's permission and his okay because if God is okay with it, then that means I will have grace to be kept safe. God said that my children will know my voice, and we know his voice because we spend time talking with our father just like you would with your natural mother and father. I spend more time talking with God than I do with people. I have come to an understanding that God is the most important thing in my life, and I will not take our relationship for granted. Now this leads me to talk about the protection that God gives to all of his warriors and future champions.

Let's take a look at the book of Ephesians chapter 6. This chapter clearly explains to us how to prepare for the lifelong spiritual battle that you will be facing as long as you reside here on earth.

Ephesians 6:10–17 talks about putting on the armor of God daily, and this is very important for the champion of God. We are to be ready day and night. The enemy does not call you to make an appointment so he can attack you. The enemy just comes when you least expect him. He comes to steal, kill, and destroy, wreaking havoc and stress to the unsuspected. So that means we are to be ready in and out of season no matter what. Literally, your life depends on you being prepared. Amen.

However, God has given us gifts of protection to fight in the spiritual battle that we can use in the natural war against flesh and blood.

The helmet of salvation

The helmet of salvation is the protector of your mind, clearly keeping your mind focused on the gift of salvation, the free gift that God gave us with no strings attached. The helmet is protection from the wicked thoughts of destruction that keep your mind off God. The wicked thoughts of destruction evolve around three things: money, lust, and envy. These three will sow discord and division and destruction in any relationship if not monitored and kept in check always.

The helmet of salvation is designed to keep you focused on God's love for you and all the wonderful things he did to show you how much he loved us. Every one of us has gone through a life-altering experience that we can share with the world, and we know in the back of our minds it was God who delivered us or has given us a second chance to get it right.

We all have heard about how God sent his only begotten son to come and suffer so that he may die for the sins of mankind. The gift was made available to everyone, even those who chose not to accept the testimony of what God did. Guess what? It's still on the table for them if they choose to accept it later. God didn't leave anyone out, so the gift of salvation is available to all those who believed that Jesus Christ was the son of God and that he came and died for our sins. Glory be to God for the helmet of salvation.

The breast plate of righteousness

The breast plate of righteousness was designed to protect your heart from evil thinking. From the heart proceeds the issues of life. An individual's thought pattern proceeds from their heart, not their mind. His or her mind is the reaction of what comes from the heart. Whether it may be good or evil, love or hate, these are issues that come from the heart, and that is why the heart need protecting at all times.

When we love someone, our actions display love. That's vice versa. Now, there will be a time in life when you will lie to yourself as well as to others. Your mouth will say one thing, but your heart is saying something different. You are protecting your feeling by being deceptive, guarding your heart from manipulation. I will not exploit manipulative actions in this book. You will have to read the next book coming. This is one of the reasons why the heart is encased inside your rib cage, away from physical harm, and the breast plate of righteousness is God's way of protecting you from spiritual harm. Safeguarding your heart to receive instructions of life and love from him so that you can display these thoughts and actions to others is the real meaning of God's love.

Gird thy loins with truth

The truth hurts most of the time, and a lot of people really don't want to hear the truth but are willing to live with and listen to lies. Deceiving oneself is more hurtful in the long run than you can ever imagine. You can find yourself never trusting anyone and hindering your own growth from not wanting to listen to anyone. But you might admire certain people and hold them on a higher pedestal, thinking that they know it all and have all of the right answers for life.

Now catch this. If the one that has been held on a pedestal knowingly commits a wrongful act, the people who have been blind to their words and actions are not only hurt and lost because they believed in the person and not in God, but they find themselves falling away from God. However, God knowing this put a secondary plan in effect. So now as one of God's champions, you have an obligation to the truth. Lying and being deceitful is forbidden. It is forbidden because there is punishment following your actions for misleading God's people.

The punishment is not withheld from you so that you may think it's okay to continue playing in the sin. You are always held accountable for your actions. The punishment is rendered to you in the natural so that all may see that God is not to be mocked. Gird your loins in truth. Walk in truth always, not allowing your feet to walk on the path of destruction. Speak in truth always; you might hurt some feelings. But I would rather hurt your feelings with truth than speak a lie to cover up the truth that will eventually be revealed at some point. Live in truth always. Shame is an embarrassment that you don't want any part of.

So allow your life to be surrounded by truth. It is whom you associate yourself with in public and out of public—your life and the affiliations that you attract—that is a reflection of your character, so being mindful of who you are and who you represent is always on the forefront of the truth in your mindset.

Keep God first, and he will keep you.

Shod my feet with the gospel of peace

The world thrives on gossip, backbiting, envy, lust, fornication, commotion, and confusion. If you can try and avoid these vicious attacks from those who are close to you, now you're getting prepared to follow the path of destiny.

When God has called you, he is going to make room in your life so that you can get your proper training. He will close doors that are meant to stay shut and open doors that were meant only for you during your training period. You don't have to worry about anything during this time. God is going to provide and separate you from the crowd so that you will not be distracted from the lesson.

You're probably asking yourself, what lesson do I need to be taught that God hasn't already revealed to me? Well, my friend, it's the lesson of walking in peace. It's a simple but tough lesson to learn. If you think about it too long, it starts to magnify itself a little bit like trigonometry.

There are a lot of people who think because they read their Bible and go to church to be seen as a Christian, they are walking in peace. I hate to bust your bubble, but peace is a lesson that must be learned just like love and long-suffering. If you are having trouble with being honest with yourself, there is a way you can learn this lesson—the right way.

Well, if I stay away from certain people, now I will have peace. Wrong. This is not peace; this is you just not wanting to be bothered with those particular individuals. If I don't do what other people do that I hear about and compare myself to them, now I have peace. Wrong. You are being a hypocrite.

Walking in peace does not give me the authority to look down on others and put myself on a pedestal in my own mind. Walking in peace is having confidence and trust in the Spirit of God living on the inside of your heart. I can't walk around thinking that I am more holy than you because I chose to keep God first. That is not what God would want.

How can you enlighten the world with love and wisdom if you are walking around thinking you are better than everyone? It's not about being better than no one; it's all about living in the world as an example of the child of God. I don't need to separate; I need to be a light in a dark world, unafraid of the world and what others are thinking and saying about me. I come in love and truth. I don't have to pretend to be better. No.

I have to show you who comes first in my life. He is the head of my life, and he makes all my decisions for me. I live my life to represent him. I feel good when I make him look good, when he gets the glory and the credit. Guess what? Now I have the peace that he promised to leave me with.

Peace comes from God, not from people or the worldly possessions that you may obtain. Peace is with you no matter what is going on around you. Peace prepares you for everything that goes on in life. That is exactly why you cannot obtain it on your own. God is peace, and when you have him with you, there is nothing that can disturb and take that away from you. Lord, continue to shod my feet with the gospel of peace.

Food for thought: The armor of God is spiritual, so in order to obtain the armor, you must have spiritual permission. And this entails having a spiritual relationship.

The shield of faith

It's just like buying a new car without insurance coverage. You have got to have insurance before you leave the parking lot. You leave the dealership in peace knowing that you are protected against unforeseen accidents.

This is how life goes. You need protection in the spiritual realm as well as in the natural. The question is how I could obtain a spiritual protection policy and how much will it cost me. Getting the spiritual protection policy that you need is the easy part; keeping your premiums paid so that your policy does not lapse is a different story.

There are three spiritual enemies that you will run into in this life that you need protection from: your own pride, lust, and doubt. If you don't have the protection against them, you will eventually fall.

In your own ability, you cannot win against these three enemies attacking you at the same time. It's hard enough to fight against them one at a time. Most people succumb to temptation when all three attack on every thought, lingering all day in battle, preventing you from eating, marching well into the night causing you to lose sleep. It will inevitably win unless you get some help. What can you do?

You can't turn to alcohol. It only worsens after you sober up. Drugs is not the answer. Friends and family who have more issues than you definitely is not the solution. Pity parties only keep me from looking in the right places for my answers. Let's cut through the woods on this one.

The shield of faith is your answer to fighting against all three of these enemies at any given time, even when they all come at once. The shield of faith was designed to block off the fiery darts—pride, worry, stress, and doubt—a spiritual defense for a spiritual offense. You don't need to pollute your body with toxins to fight in the spiritual realm. You need the spiritual armor and the spiritual guidance to win against the spiritual attacks from the spiritual enemy.

How can you get a spiritual policy? Simple. Just ask for one. And what is the cost? Spending time with God daily whether it be reading his word, praising him, listening to gospel music, and being thankful. This is how you pay on your spiritual policy, and your premium will never go unpaid. God will do the rest.

The sword of God

Last but not least, I need the sword. I can use the sword in the spiritual as well as in the natural realm. The double-edged sword cuts through bone and marrow, spirit and flesh, family and friends. The sword is to be practiced with daily so that you may know how to use it in the day of battle. And believe me, once you pick up the sword, the battle is on the way.

So you might as well get your training started and train as though your life depended on it because it does. And when that time comes to do battle, your training is going to reveal who you are and what you're made of. The Bible says the battle is the Lord, but guess what? God isn't the one who is being attacked. He is the one whom you call on for help in the battle, and he needs you to be prepared to fight the battle.

Some of you might think that all you have to do is call on God and sit back with your feet up because you know God is going to fight the battle for you. Wrong again. God wants you to do something besides sit back with your feet up. He wants you to put on the armor, and that shows him you are ready to do battle and not just a couch potato. God loves a champion. They are the ones he chose; he knew they were not afraid to fight in the battle if they had to.

How can I get the spiritual armor? Simple. Spend time with God and allow him to train you, and he will send you in the direction to be around others who are in training or who have been trained and have now been put in position to be trainers. Glory be to God.

The armor of God is spiritual, and the attacks from the enemy are spiritual at first and then transform over into the natural where it is openly seen. So the battle starts in the spiritual, and that's where we want it to end. Get your victory in the spiritual realm, and it will also manifest into the natural. You have to put yourself in a position to be able to defend yourself and your loved ones. There might be a time when you can't call on someone to do battle with you—pray for you—so you got to go in alone. That's where you will find God. When you think you are alone, he is right there beside you on the battlefield.

Prayer warriors

When I need a prayer heard and answered, I need it. I don't want to have any doubt that it's not getting heard or answered. So I keep God first in my life, and my circle of friends filled with prayer warriors. I work hard living for God, and so do my circle of friends— real friends that I did not choose for myself but God chose for me.

We don't talk as often as we can, but through the spirit, our love for God is rock-solid. We love, honor, and serve God with the utmost respect. Jesus Christ is the Lord over our lives.

Never will I expect to receive a call of bashing others, looking down on others, entangling with gossip, and twisting the word of God to benefit our own selfish desires. I accept God's chosen friends for me as my lifelong friends, and I thank God for the love of the spirit that each one of you treasure, not just for the words you speak but your actions of love and zeal for God.

I need not put anyone on blast, but you know who you are. Without you ever knowing, you made it possible by assisting me in writing this book with your words of encouragement. So I thank God for you all, and may the Lord continue to bless you and shine his spirit down and through you. Prayer warriors for life!

A L O N E R

Now this might be the shortest chapter in the book because it is exactly what the title says—walking all alone. As you may already know, there are rules in every aspect of life, and believe it or not, there are rules to walking alone. First of all, walking alone requires you not to be afraid to leave the past behind you (toxic memories, relationships, friends, and sometimes family). Secondly, walking alone requires of you letting go of your own selfish ambitions, admitting to yourself that you need help finding the road to your destiny. Third but not least, I need change in my life, and that requires me letting go of my old ways of looking at everything and allowing my mindset to accept change.

Food for thought: True happiness is not in the natural.

Walking alone, you are going to obtain a new mindset, and if you will stay on the path, then you are going to find yourself heading in a new direction in life. It will be new and strange at first, and definitely lonely, because you don't know what to expect. But fret not because you are there for a reason, and guess what? It was meant for you to be heading that way alone without all the answers and no assistance from the past.

I can tell you from personal experience what you can expect on your journey that everyone is going to go through, learning new lessons and gaining new experiences. I would advise you to pay attention on the journey. The answers to your questions and doubts will come in simple form, nothing lit up on a billboard sign but very simple and plain. So pay close attention because the test comes later.

If I could give you all the answers to your questions, situations, and what to expect, I probably wouldn't do it. Not that I wouldn't want to help, but this is your journey and you have to walk it alone. You're going to learn to be a thinking individual, accepting what it is you can change, and leaving the rest alone. You're going to learn to speak only when it's needed. Being a good listener is where you are going to find a lot of answers to questions in life in general. You're going to learn how to pay attention to the spirit of others, not the words that they speak but the aura of how their spirit presents itself to you. And that's when you'll learn to keep it moving.

It's so mind blowing how we think that we really need to be around people all the time; but in fact, we only need to be around people for celebrations, work, and a little social gathering. I don't need my space constantly crowded all day, every single day of the year.

Most people feel as though they need attention all the time, just like a newborn baby, and really wouldn't know how to function if they weren't seeking attention all the time.

This will be one of the hardest lesson to learn if you are always concerned about being in the mix of the action—letting go of the action.

Food for thought: Attention seekers think

> *I need to be seen. I need to be heard. I need to let everyone know all my business. I sometimes need to expose other people's faults and shortcoming just to get some attention.*

Okay, we get it. So you like attention, and that is good if it's for the right reason.

Here is an exercise that I would dare you to partake. Take a peak in the mirror and look into the eyes of the individual that you see in the mirror, and be honest with yourself. Are you okay with yourself? Would you deal with a person like you?

This is how I had to examine myself, and I found out that I could deal with a person like me. I wouldn't have to worry about walking alone and unable to trust anyone because of selfish flaws (backbiting, greed, envy, jealousy, lust). It requires being honest and disciplined to yourself, to not have to lie to yourself. Don't beat yourself up too bad. It took a long time for me to get to know myself, and appreciate who I am, and not be afraid of hiding a dark side that I had to let go in order to move forward.

Walking alone can bring out the worst in a person, or it can be a medicine to help accomplish whatever goal you are trying to reach. The fact of the matter is, if you actually focus on walking alone, doors of opportunity will present themselves to you. You don't have to run around in circles looking for the Scooby snack. Stay focused and dedicate yourself to yourself.

Blessings to your new assignment, and favor allows others to help you in a way that you couldn't help yourself (letting go of pride). Now I would like to encourage you with my own testimony. Right now in the midst of writing this book, only a few people knew of my desire to be a writer. I tried my hand in a lot of different tasks that ended up with me being frustrated with the people I chose to bring aboard, and myself for wasting time on a dead-end task. But everyone thinks that their venture is the take off to finding the pot of gold or something to that effect. Well, I finally gave up on chasing my dream, and I asked God to reveal to me what it is he had planned for me when I was told to write this book.

I told no one about my vision. I didn't want anyone asking any questions or try to give negative feedback of discouragement. I didn't want anyone praying for me or praying against me because in my heart, I knew they probably would not have understood the vision that God gave me. So I kept it to myself until God was ready for me to reveal it to the world.

So now, I was back at square one trying to do something that I had never done or had an interest of doing, but this time, it was different and it felt different. I was actually overcome with peace. I didn't have to answer to anyone, I wasn't responsible for anyone else's livelihood, and I didn't have to put my trust in other people to write what was coming through me.

Now that is when I knew my assignment was to be a writer, and God chose me to be one of his champions in this era. As the time went by and I started to see blank pages being filled with words of encouragement, I had to be alone to get it done. This was my lesson that was being taught to me; and I had to receive it, learn it, and apply it in order for me to see the results of me being on the path of my destiny.

We all have our own destiny, and some will find theirs and others might not. But the lesson of being a loner is sometimes a heart-breaker when you don't feel the support that you think you deserve and you should be getting. But it's not coming your way. It actually took everything in me to be quiet and stay focused to be able to write. It was days, sometimes weeks, when the motivation to write would come. I could hear doubt and lack of confidence through the halls of my own home, my mind being attacked by the enemy of doubt, trying to get me to give up on my writing and let the vision slowly die. But I thank God that the vision that he gave me was stronger than my own will to just settle and be happy for what he had already blessed me with, and to be content.

I wanted more. I felt as though my life wasn't being fulfilled. I wasn't lacking for anything, but I wasn't enjoying life like I knew I was supposed to be enjoying it. I always felt something was off. Something was missing. And the more I tried to explain it to my wife, it just seemed I wasn't getting through to her. She was content with me working and paying the bills and going to church with her on Sundays, but she couldn't understand that I wanted more than the routine lifestyle that we had grown accustomed to living.

Sometimes, I would think she just didn't understand how bad I wanted to find my gift and fulfill my destiny, but I thank God for filling in the empty space in my life that I was trying so hard to fill in. I really wanted to know, was God with me or was it me on a selfish roller-coaster ride? So I put everything on hold just to spend time with my writing, concentrating on nothing and no one during my writing time. I would turn my phones off and no television. I even stopped attending church just for a season so that I could get all the available time and space that was allotted to me while my wife was away—quiet time that I felt I needed without any distraction.

I would talk briefly about the book sometimes, but I felt I wasn't getting the enthusiastic response from my wife like the way I felt about the book. I am not saying she wasn't happy for me writing the book, but I felt at the time she should have been happier for me than I was. But that was a lesson to learn. Everyone is not going to see your gift until God reveals it to be seen. So I stopped talking about it and focused on finishing it so that I could get it done to my publisher.

Now mind you, I am not saying that I love my wife any less because she didn't see the gift. No, it just wasn't the right time to be seen. Plus God wanted me to stay focused and not think about being patted on the back for something I had not done. Believe me, this has made me stronger in the belief of my God-given vision. So I said that to say this: everyone isn't going to see what God is doing at the time he is working with you. And it's up to you to stay focused, stay quiet, stay mild mannered, and keep it moving while God is busy with you. Remember, it might only feel lonely at the time you are going through it, but you are never really alone. And it's only a lesson that you have got to learn and master to be able to perform at your best when you need to.

As a champion, you are going to have more lonely days than you can ever imagine. All the excitement that comes with being a champion is going to wear on you over time so you have to learn how to separate and walk alone.

Recharge your battery

The work that you have got to put in to become a champion is almost the same amount required to maintain your sanity, and it does require the same amount of rest to recharge your battery sometimes a little longer.

Getting your proper rest is important. Allowing your mind to rest is key to your longevity. As long as you can think on it, you can find the right pieces to bring together to keep winning.

I must admit walking alone is a lonely journey, a journey not everyone is willing to partake. But from personal experience, I will say success is truly hidden on the path that is less traveled. In order to walk alone, you have got to possess the right tools to carry with you on the journey. And the reason why I said *tools* is that you are going to have to do some work on the journey.

The tools you are going to need are a hammer, a screwdriver, and pliers; and with those tools you will also need common sense, self-motivation, and a spiritual foundation. Yes, you are going to need God because it's going to be a lot of lonely days and nights, and you're going to need someone to talk with. Know he wouldn't leave you while you are on this journey.

Walking alone means no one gets to come on this journey with you. How long will this journey last? No one knows that either. But whatever it is that has you following the path of walking alone, always remember where you came from and stay focused on where you are trying to go. Let the spirit guide you forevermore.

THINKERS

The world is under the assumption that the strong is who will survive. Now this may be truth in the animal kingdom, but in the world we live and function in today, that is part truth. We live in a society where ideas are brought into functioning reality and implemented into our everyday lives as a means of survival and social interaction. Thinkers are who make the world evolve into the next plateau of reality. However, we are going to do a spin-off in this last chapter. We are going to explore three types of thinkers and how they perform to get the job done.

As one of God's champions or future champions, you have already assessed that thinking is one of your greatest assets that you will be applying and defending all of your days. Next to having faith, thinking is all you truly own, and it's the only thing you will be able to take with you into the next life. The gift of thinking is divine, and yes it came from God. If you may have forgotten, God did create everything from his majestic and supreme thinking especially when he thought to create man in his own likeness and image. So we did receive some of his thinking attribute but only to a certain degree.

God spread out the power of thinking over time so that the world would evolve in each era of time as you see it today—not too fast and certainly not too slow. Each era also would have to inherit a few of God's champions groomed just for that era to keep God lifted up and the people from forgetting who he is and where they came from. We follow an A-list of chosen champions, and I am grateful and truly honored that God chose me to represent him and the kingdom in this era.

New-age champions is who we are, and we represent God in the order that he would like us to present ourselves to continue to draw

58

others to him. Now on your journey of walking alone, practice on your thinking and chewing bubble gum—yes, walking and chewing gum. The lesson is learning to stay focused on your thinking while you are walking and chewing bubble gum. It's a gift to be able to do all three and speak in detail of each one and still perform in an assigned task. Being able to multitask (think chess thinking) and stay focused while life is still going on around you—believe it or not, not everyone is willing to do it. There are three types of thinkers. Which one are you? Keep it to yourself and ask God to continue to give you growth in your category.

Over-the-top thinkers are idealists. They are abstract creative thinkers who never really have the time to focus on the present but always look ahead for the new.

Mild-mannered thinkers are the go-getters. They are the producers, scriptwriters, publishers, book writers, brick-and-mortar storefront owners. They are the ones that make the over-the-top thinkers' ideas a reality.

Passive thinkers are the consumers. We accept the ideas, we buy the material, and we support the vision.

No matter the category you are presently in, you are an asset in the kingdom of God, and most of you might possess an enormous amount of strength in two or maybe all three categories. But it does no one any good if you are not using it in its intended purpose. Thinkers are always thinking no matter what time or day. You can always catch us spending our time sharpening the gift that was given from God. Spending my time with God is personal. He keeps me thinking. Keeping God first he keeps me focused on his plan and not my own.

Food for thought: Iron sharpens iron.

Thinkers tend to align themselves with thinkers alike, and growth is found in the counsel of wise thinkers. Just as I mentioned in an earlier chapter about examining yourself, examine your associates. Can I grow in this relationship? (Only you can answer this one.) As for myself, if I cannot see the growth, you can believe it will be a distant relationship. There is nothing wrong with keeping your inner circle filled with wisdom and truth. However, if you are the wisest individual in your circle, maybe it is time to incorporate some new members. Updated information goes good with the changing time. No one is using rotary dial phones anymore. The cell phone is the update, so we keep our wisdom and truth updated as well.

Every one of us has a capacity level in thinking, and not all of us are on the same level. But that does not mean you are less appreciated because of your slower thinking capacity. Once again, I must testify of my own shortcomings. I am slow in the area of common sense. I mean green as the summer grass. I couldn't get it right if my life depended on me getting it right.

But God had a plan for me, so he kept me safe while I tried my best to learn common sense. God separated me from those who were trying to use me, and he told me that I was trying too hard to fit in with a crowd that didn't mean me no good. And guess what? Years later, I am where I am today without the nonsense and shenanigans from those who really wanted to see me down and out.

So I can tell you from personal experience that God has a bigger plan for you and he already has the people in place that are going to come aboard and assist you in your area of thinking through wise counsel. This will be the time you will be learning how to think like a champion, staying focused like a champion, learning whom to trust, and learning the real meaning of patience. So we will be ending the chapter with a word of encouragement. Keep God first and he will keep you.

C O N C L U S I O N

In closing, I would like to take the time out and give a shout-out to God and my Lord and Savior Jesus Christ. And I thank the Holy Spirit for the assistance of helping me with the writing of my first book. I would like to thank each of you for taking this walk with me in the reading of my first and many more books to come. I hope that I have enlightened you in areas that were unknown or just put on the back burner of your thinking, and hopefully I have sparked a fire in the sleeping champion that is ready to face the world on your own destined journey. We need more champion laborers in this day and time than we've ever needed them. I pray that I didn't offend anyone with the truth. However, if you have any questions or concerns, please feel free to contact me at tonydrakeministries@ gmail.com.

ABOUT THE AUTHOR

Born and raised in Benton Harbor, Michigan the oldest of four boys and currently residing in the mid western state of Missouri. Married with 4 boys of my own and pursuing my life long dream of becoming a best selling author. Keeping God first is the light of my existence without him nothing positive would have come into fruition concerning my life. I am compelled to live my life as a servant of the Lord without him I am nothing so I give the glory and honor to him for all that he has done and continues to do in and through me. As God leads the way my life will be revealed throughout the forth coming books my journey has been a long hard road and I'm not going to waste precious time patting myself on the back when the glory belongs to God.

Tony Drake

CPSIA information can be obtained
at www.ICGtesting.com
Printed in the USA
LVHW012300190122
708244LV00006B/25

9 781638 747482